MONTANA
impressions

photography by John Lambing

FARCOUNTRY
PRESS

Right: Ear Mountain on the Rocky
Mountain Front.

Title page: On the Yellowstone River
near Forsyth.

Front cover: Below some of Montana's high-
est peaks, the Beartooth Mountains.

Back cover: The promise of a storm rises
over south-central Montana.

ISBN: 1-56037-196-X
Photographs © 2001 by John Lambing
© 2001 Farcountry Press

For more information on our books write: Farcountry Press,
P.O. Box 5630, Helena, MT 59604 or call: (800) 654-1105 or visit
www.montanamagazine.com

Created, produced, and designed in the United States.
Printed in Korea

Right: Gorge Creek in the East Pioneer Mountains.

Facing page: Looking down into Boulder Creek Valley from Glacier National Park's Siyeh Pass.

Right: Day begins on the Upper Missouri near Craig.

Below: Arnica, paintbrush, and geranium brighten Montana summers.

Above: Old homestead buildings on a Granite County ranch.

Facing page: The Tongue River flows through its southeastern Montana canyon.

Above: Beside the Missouri River, a train heads north toward the Golden Triangle.

Left: Townsend's tree-lined streets begin to change into autumn garb.

Above: Roundup Rapids awaits some Blackfoot River rafters.

Facing page: Lima Peaks in southwest Montana.

Above: A prairie church in Hill County.

Facing page: The promise of a storm rises over south-central Montana.

Above: Across the Clearwater River near Seeley Lake.

Facing page: Early autumn frost chills the Garden Wall, Glacier National Park.

Above: Some of Montana's best rangeland lies below the Bridger Mountains.

Facing page: Frosty sonata along the North Fork of the Blackfoot River.

Above: Solid log construction holds up on this Crazy Mountains barn.

Facing page: Liberty County wheatfield.

Cracker Lake *(above)* and Grizzly Lake *(facing page)* are jewels to be discovered by Glacier National Park hikers.

Above: In the Fort Benton area, Goose Bill Butte and straw ready for winter.

Facing page: Tiber Reservoir lies below a fierce sunset.

Above: Brilliantly colored poplar leaves afloat.

Right: Pausing just for a moment in their round of frantic traveling, a clan of chipmunks.

Facing page: Lewis and Clark named this river "Philanthropy" for one of President Jefferson's virtues; later prospectors tagged it the Stinkingwater, but today it's known as the Ruby.

Left: Arrowleaf balsamroot below the Absaroka Mountains.

Facing page: Muddy from its journey across open plains, the Marias River flows near Shelby.

29

Above: Prairie rattlers are one of Montana's common snakes.

Right: Bison in the tens of thousands once caused the prairie below the Rocky Mountain Front to shake as they ran by.

Left: Winter mist rises through Yellowstone National Park.

Facing page: On the Flathead Indian Reservation, the Flathead River flows beneath the Mission Mountains.

Right: Prairie abloom near Heart Butte.

Below: Early snow temporarily clothes the "Sleeping Giant" that lies on Helena's northern horizon.

Above: Lady slippers.

Facing page: Cobalt sky + emerald grass + turquoise water = Glacier National Park.

Above: Haystack Buttes in the Terry Badlands hold layers of silt from vanished ancient lakebeds.

Facing page: After the wheat harvest, near Cut Bank.

Left: Calypso orchids also are known as fairy slippers.

Below: Horsemint and fleabane.

Facing page: The Salish Mountains near Polson.

Above: Montana ranks in the top five states in wheat production.

Facing page: Grain elevators near Hobson stand at attention to greet a new day.

Right: Rainbow trout are a favorite for state anglers.

Below: Looking through a natural arch into southeastern Montana's Bighorn Canyon.

Facing page: A blue-and-white day in Gallatin River Canyon.

Above: Patterns of sunlight and wood grain on an old barn near Manhattan.

Facing page: The Jefferson River snakes through Madison County shortly before joining the Madison and the Gallatin to form the Mighty Mo.

Above: The beautiful Swan Valley spreads out below the Swan Range.

Facing page: A peaceful early-summer day along the Flathead River.

Above: The rugged Spanish Peaks rise near Bozeman.

Left: The Snowcrest Range in southwestern Montana reaches 10,600 feet in elevation.

Above: A rollercoaster route to the Mission Mountains.

Facing page: Classic barn red backed by the Bridger Mountains.

Left: Glacier National Park's Baring Creek.

Facing page: Belt Creek flows near Monarch.

Above: Mule deer pose for a silhouette portrait.

Right: One way to enjoy north-central Montana's Bearpaw Mountains.

Above: Early morning in the Bridger Range.

Facing page: A combine waits out winter in a Cascade County wheat field.

Above: Mama mountain goat and kid.

Facing page: Tendoy Lake reflects the Pioneer Mountains.

Above: St. Mary Falls in Glacier National Park.

Left: Fireweed, a colonizer after forest fires, blooms near Cooke City north of Yellowstone National Park.

Above: Wild lightning on the prairie near Jordan.

Facing page: Hay's in for this Stanford-area ranch.

Left: Wildfires color the dawn sky near Hysham on the Yellowstone River.

Facing page: A daytime moon rises over red clover and the Crazy Mountains.

Above: Jerusalem Rocks stand outside of Sweetgrass near the Canadian border.

Facing page: The White Cliffs along the Wild and Scenic section of the upper Missouri reminded early visitors of castles and fortresses.

Above: Waiting for the long-gone train in Meagher County.

Left: Wild iris dots the prairie below Birdtail Butte, west of Cascade.

Above: Fog turned to frost decorates French Creek near Anaconda.

Facing page: Bull Mountain above the Boulder River Valley.

Above: Near Valier, the pot of gold is the crop in this wheat field.

Left: Abandoned corral in the Bearpaw Mountains.

Above: Larch along Lake Alva show their autumn gold below the Swan Range.

Facing page: One-time homestead below the Mission Mountains.

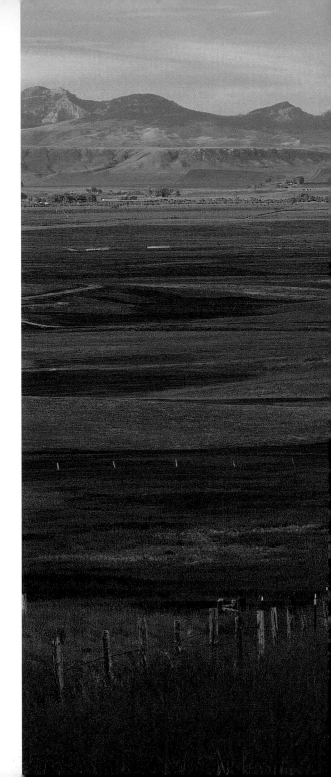

Right: Looking to Crown Butte from Greenfields Bench near Simms.

Below: A sugarbowl blossom.

Along the Rocky Mountain Front,
where mountains meet plains.

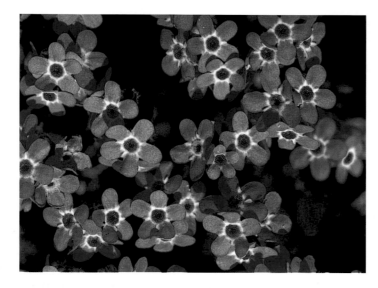

Above: Alpine forget-me-not.

Right: Wildhorse Island on Flathead Lake.

Above: In the Marias River Valley.

Facing page: Hot and dry near Mizpah, Powder River Valley.

Above: A grand old barn near Fort Benton.

Facing page: Leading on to White Sulphur Springs.

Above: Freezeout Lake settles in for the night.

Facing page: Autumn brilliance lights the Jefferson River and the Tobacco Root Mountains.

Above: At Melville, below the Crazy Mountains.

Facing page: Sixteenmile Creek meets the swollen Missouri River near Toston and a bridge to nowhere.

Beaverhead County Ranch.

Above: Before they had horses, Native Americans hazed bison herds off cliffs like this one near Simms, camping below to butcher and preserve the meat.

Facing page: Middle Fork, Judith River, in the Little Belt Mountains.

John Lambing is a hydrologist with the U.S. Geological Survey in Helena who spends much of his off-work time roaming the Montana countryside in search of interesting and beautiful landscape images. Originally from St. Louis, Missouri, he has lived in Montana since 1981 and has been exploring the west ever since. John's photos have been regularly published in *Montana Magazine*, *Montana Outdoors*, and numerous other regional publications.

His photography favors expansive wide-open areas that maintain much of their original native character. John enjoys nature photography because he feels that merging the technical elements of the camera with the visual beauty of the land provides a perfect balance between intellectual stimulation and artistic appreciation. Whether observing the geologic and climatic forces at work on the landscape or witnessing stunning scenes of color and light, sublimely composed by nature, he believes the journey to a potential photo is always worth the trip.